Contents

Some words are shown in bold, **like this**. You can find them in the glossary on page 23.

What is football?

Football is a game we play with a ball. People play football all around the world.

Sport and My Body

Football

Charlotte Guillain

www.raintreepublishers.co.uk
Visit our website to find out
more information about
Raintree books.

To order:
☎ Phone +44 (0) 1865 888066
🖹 Fax +44 (0) 1865 314091
🖳 Visit www.raintreepublishers.co.uk

Raintree is an imprint of Capstone Global Library
Limited, a company incorporated in England and Wales
having its registered office at 7 Pilgrim Street, London,
EC4V 6LB – Registered company number: 6695582

Text © Capstone Global Library Limited 2009
First published in hardback in 2009
First published in paperback in 2010
The moral rights of the proprietor have been asserted.

Edited by Siân Smith, Rebecca Rissman, and
Charlotte Guillain
Designed by Joanna Hinton-Malivoire
Picture research by Ruth Blair
Production by Duncan Gilbert
Originated by Chroma Graphics (Overseas) Pte. Ltd
Printed and bound in China by South China Printing
Company Ltd

ISBN 978 1 406 21112 2 (hardback)
13 12 11 10 09
10 9 8 7 6 5 4 3 2 1

ISBN 978 1 406 21118 4 (paperback)
14 13 12 11 10
10 9 8 7 6 5 4 3 2 1

British Library Cataloguing in Publication Data
Guillain, Charlotte.
    Football. -- (Sport and my body)
    1. Soccer--Physiological aspects--Juvenile literature.
    2. Soccer--Social aspects--Juvenile literature.
    I. Title II. Series
    613.7'11-dc22

Acknowledgements
We would like to thank the following for permission
to reproduce photographs: Alamy p.**15** (© Christina
Ferrin); Corbis pp.**4** (Christian Liewig), **5** (Marcus
Brandt/dpa), **6** (Kevin Dodge), **8** (Ned Frisk
Photography), **9** (Jim Cummins), **11** (Fancy/Veer),
17 (MM Productions), **19** (Jon Feingersh/zefa), **20**
(Wolfgang Flamisch/zefa), **23** (MM Productions),
23 (Marcus Brandt/dpa); Getty Images pp.**10** (Amy
Guip/Photographer's Choice), **12** (Anita van Zyl/
Gallo Images), **16** (Andrew Olney/Stone), **18**, **23**
(Brad Wilson); iStockphoto pp.**22**, **22**, **22**, **14** (©
Matthew Ragen), **22**, **23** (© Oktay Ortakcioglu);
Photolibrary p.**21** (Monkey Business Images Ltd); p.**7**,
23 (© Digital Vision); Science Photo Library pp.**13**, **23**
(GUSTOIMAGES).
Cover photograph of a football being kicked reproduced
with permission of Punchstock/Brand X Pictures. Back
cover images reproduced with permission of iStockphoto:
1. whistle; 2. shin pads (© Oktay Ortakcioglu).

Every effort has been made to contact copyright holders
of material reproduced in this book. Any omissions will
be rectified in subsequent printings if notice is given to
the publishers.

Disclaimer
All the Internet addresses (URLs) given in this book were
valid at the time of going to press. However, due to the
dynamic nature of the Internet, some addresses may
have changed, or sites may have changed or ceased to
exist since publication. While the author and publisher
regret any inconvenience this may cause readers, no
responsibility for any such changes can be accepted by
either the author or the publisher.

Some people play football for a team. Some people play football with their friends.

How do I learn to play football?

You can learn to play football in a park or a playground. All you need is a ball and a few friends.

You might play football at school, or in a club. A **coach** or teacher will help you.

How do I use my legs and feet?

You use your legs to run when you play football. You use your feet to **control** the ball.

You use your feet to **tackle** other players and get the ball. You kick the ball with your feet and sometimes you can score a goal.

How do I use my arms and hands?

Goalkeepers use their hands to save or catch the ball. They can stop other players scoring a goal.

Other players can throw the ball back from the edge of the pitch. Otherwise they should not touch the ball with their hands when they play.

How do I use the rest of my body?

You can use your head to **control** the ball. You can also use your head to pass the ball to another player, or even shoot into the goal.

You can also use your chest to control the ball. It is easier to keep control of the ball if you watch it closely.

What happens to my body when I play football?

When you play football you will start to feel warm and sweaty. You will also feel thirsty.

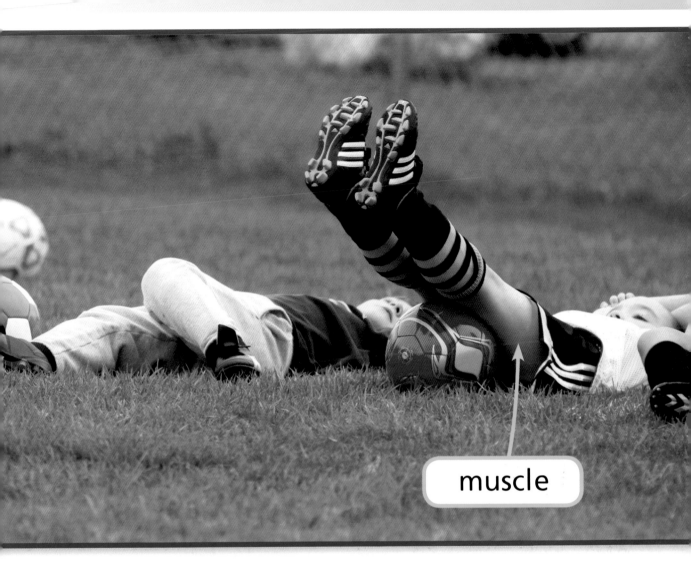

muscle

Your heart will beat faster and you will breathe more quickly. The **muscles** in your legs might ache and feel tired.

How does it feel to play football?

It is great to be part of a team.
It is a good feeling when you win
a game together.

You can make new friends when you
play football. It is fun to play together
outside in the fresh air.

How do I stay safe playing football?

You should always warm up properly before you play football. This gets your **muscles** ready to play and stops you getting hurt. You can also wear **shin pads** to stay safe.

You should always follow the rules and listen to your **coach** or the **referee**. They want to keep the players safe.

Does playing football make me healthy?

Football is good exercise and will help to keep you fit. You should also eat healthy food and drink plenty of water.

To stay healthy you need to get plenty of rest. Then you can have fun in many different ways.

Football equipment

football

football boots

shin pads

whistle

Glossary

 **coach** trainer. A coach helps people to learn and become better at something.

 **control** when you have control over something you can make it move the way you want it to

 **muscle** part of your body that helps you to move. Exercise can make muscles bigger and stronger.

 **referee** person in charge of making sure that players in a game follow the rules

 **shin pad** safety equipment players wear to protect their shins. Your shin is the front part of your leg below the knee.

 **tackle** to try and take the ball away from another player

Index

Find out more

http://www.footy4kids.co.uk
This website has lots of games for you to play to help you learn about football.

http://www.fifa.com/worldcup/index.html
Find out about the football World Cup, including photos and information about the teams.